First published 1986 by Walker Books Ltd
87 Vauxhall Walk, London SE11 5HJ

This edition produced 2000 for
The Book People Ltd, Hall Wood Avenue
Haydock, St Helens WA11 9UL

Printed in Hong Kong

ISBN 0-7445-0644-1

SHAPES

ROSALINDA KIGHTLEY

TED SMART

circle

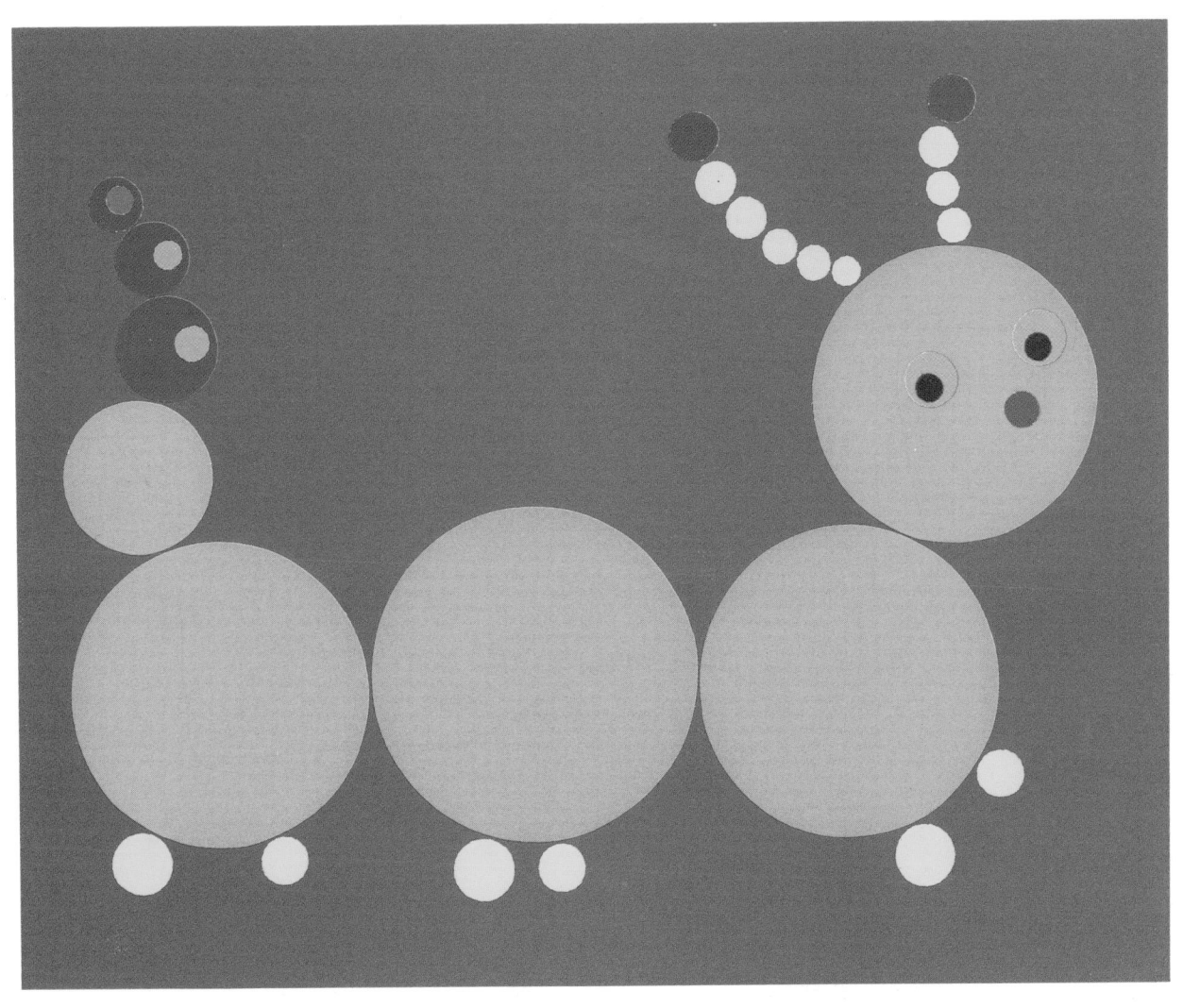

How many circles can you find?

square

How many squares can you find?

rectangle

How many rectangles can you find?

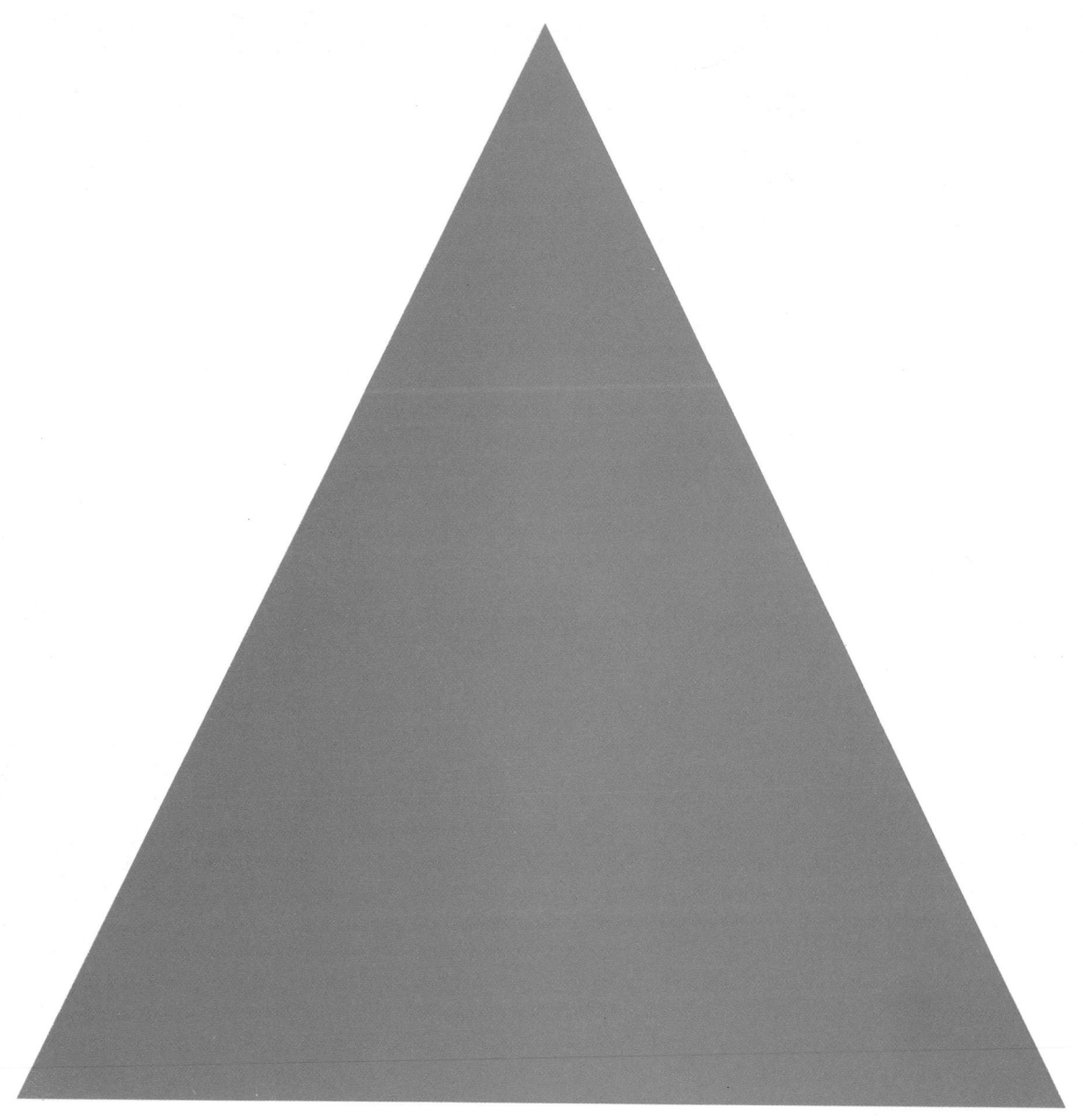

triangle

How many triangles can you find?

diamond

How many diamonds can you find?

semicircle

How many semicircles can you find?

straight line

How many straight lines can you find?

corner

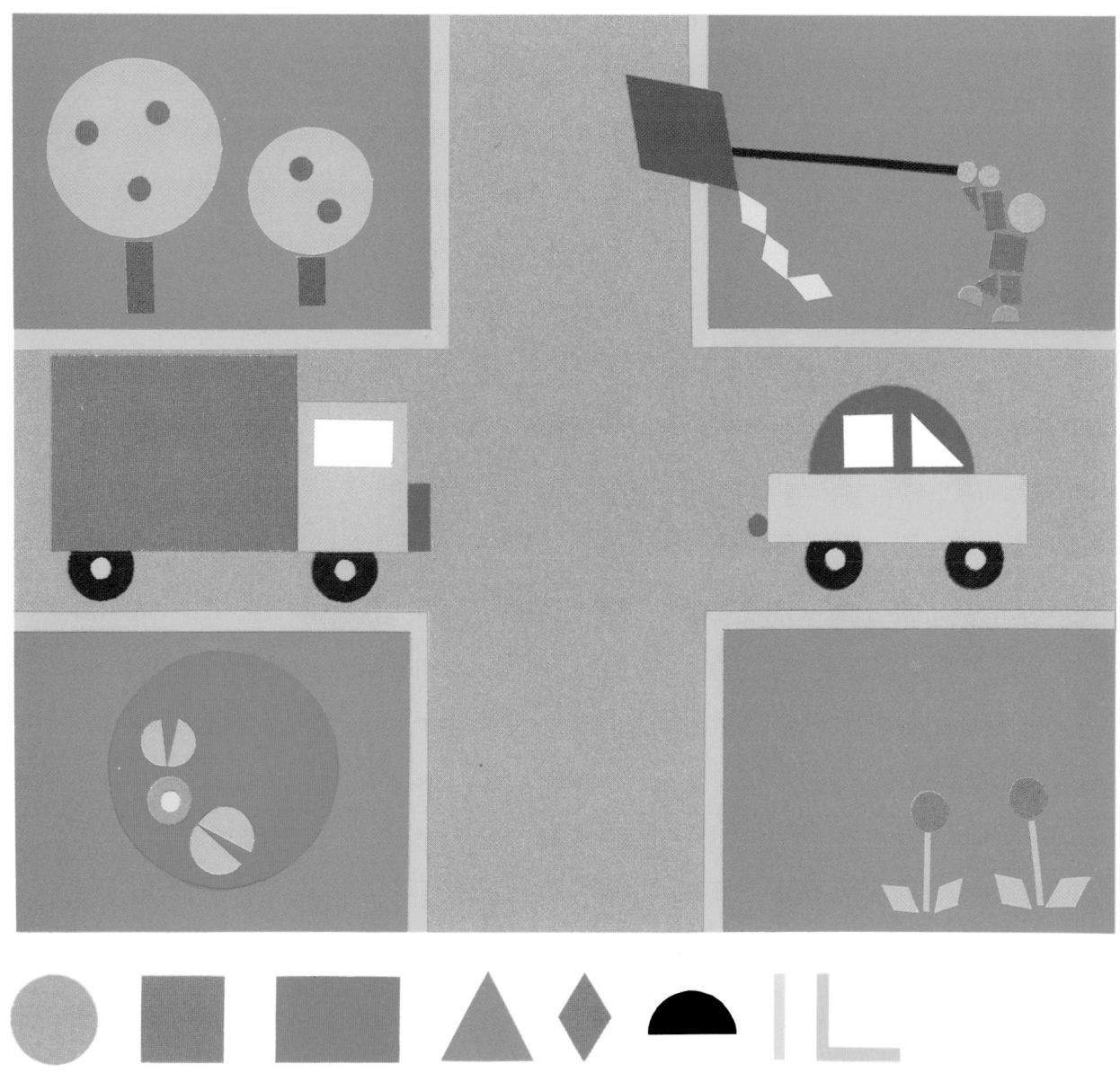

How many corners can you find?

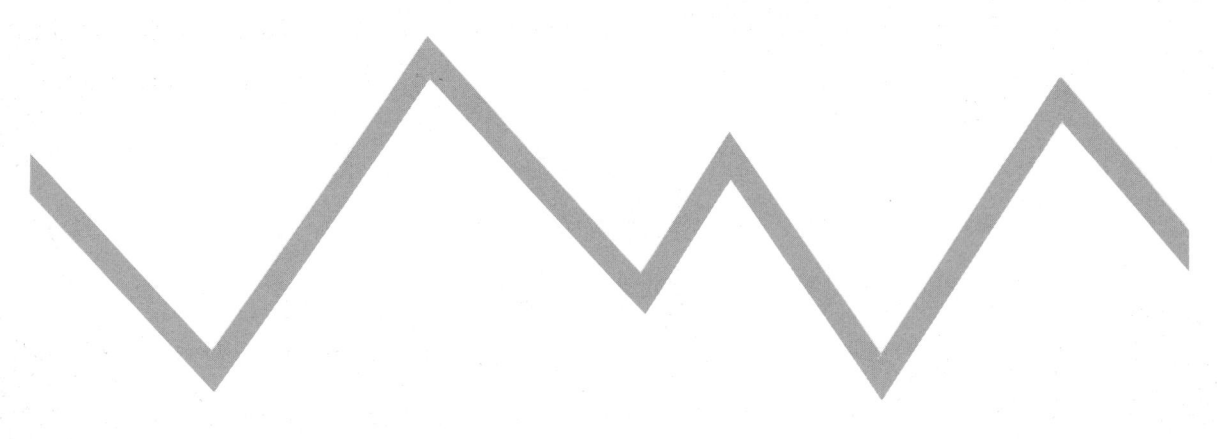

zigzag line

How many zigzag lines can you find?

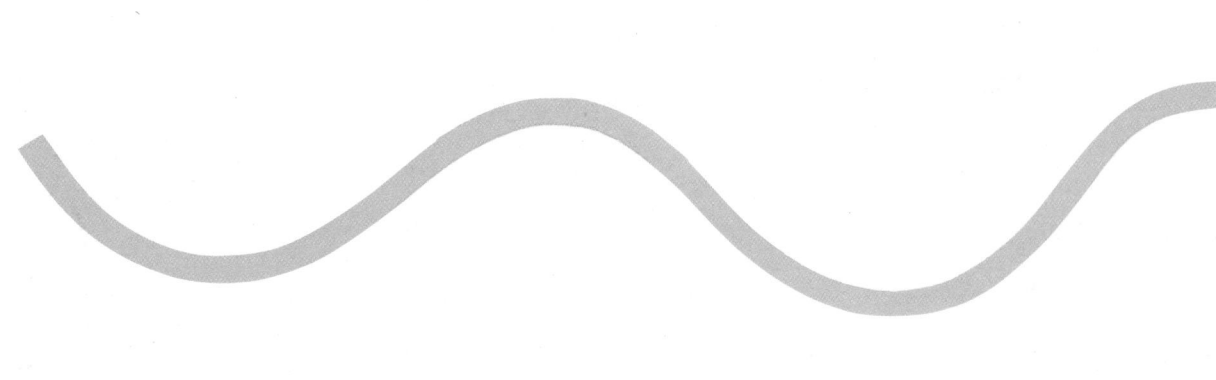

wavy line

How many wavy lines can you find?

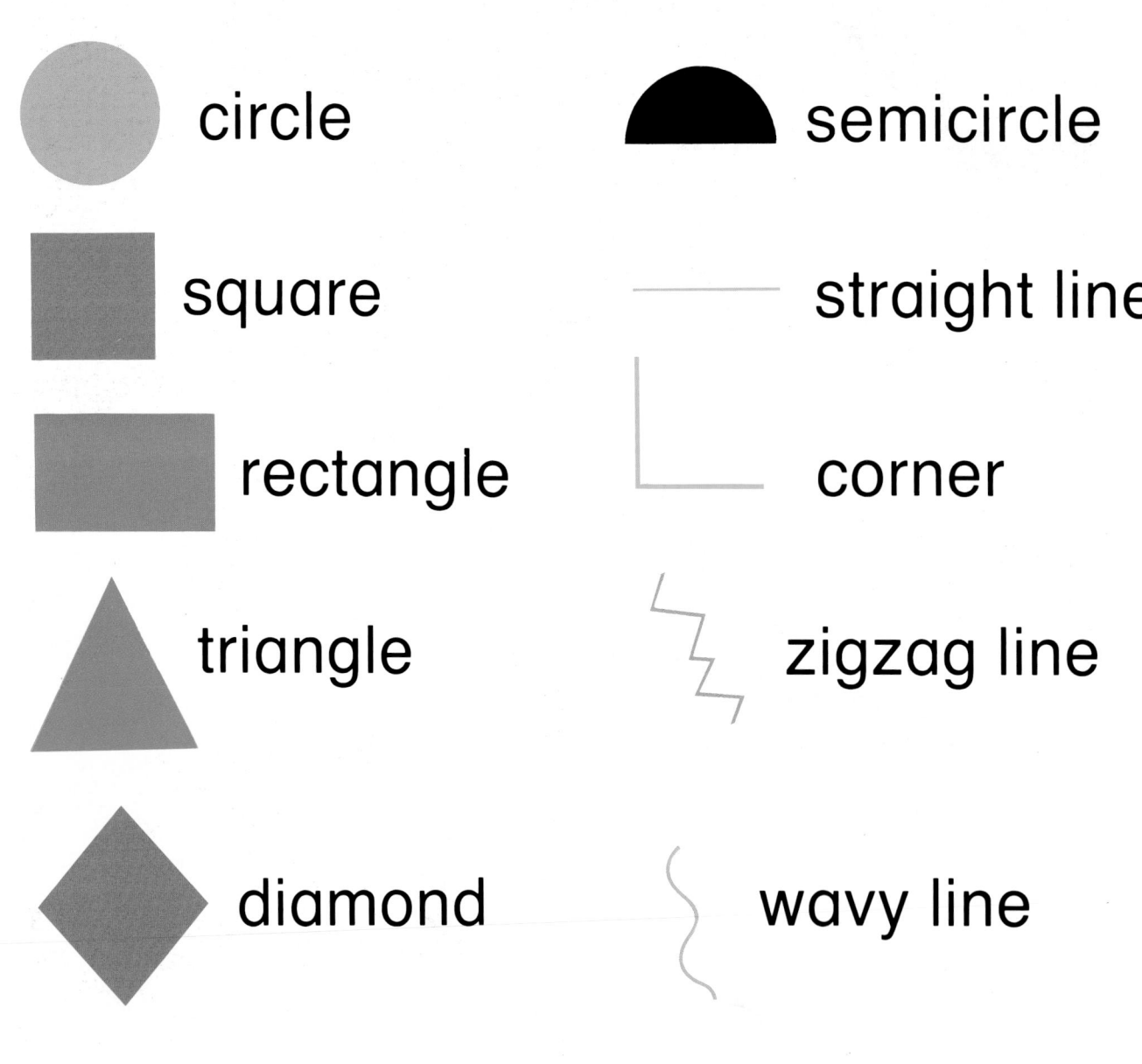

circle

semicircle

square

straight line

rectangle

corner

triangle

zigzag line

diamond

wavy line

How many shapes can you find?

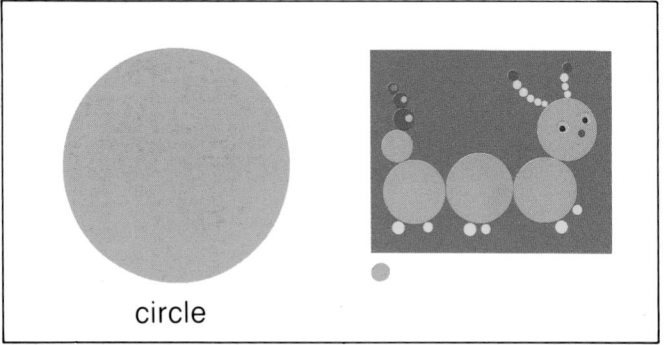

circle

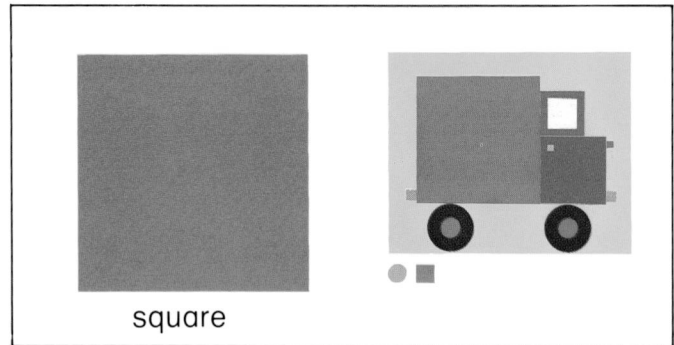

square

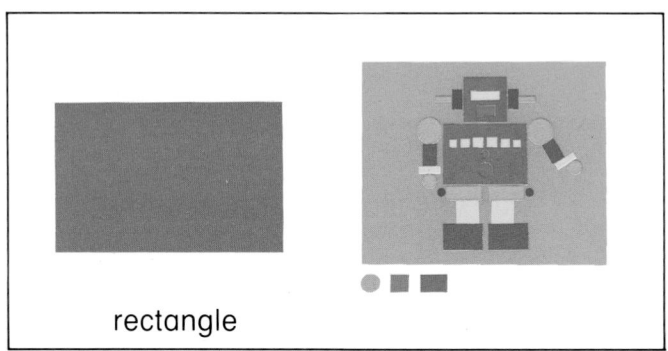

rectangle

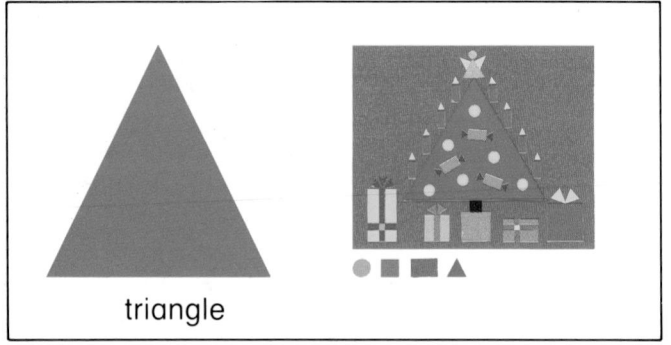

triangle

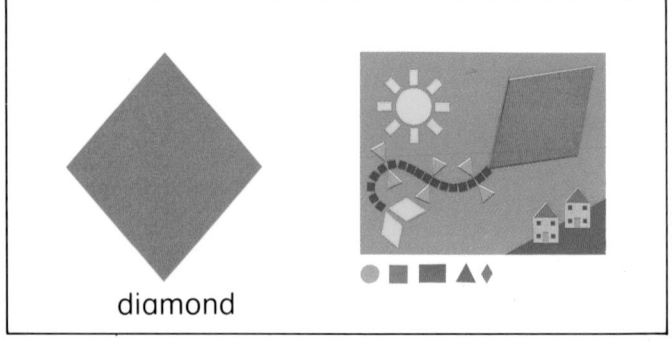

diamond

semicircle

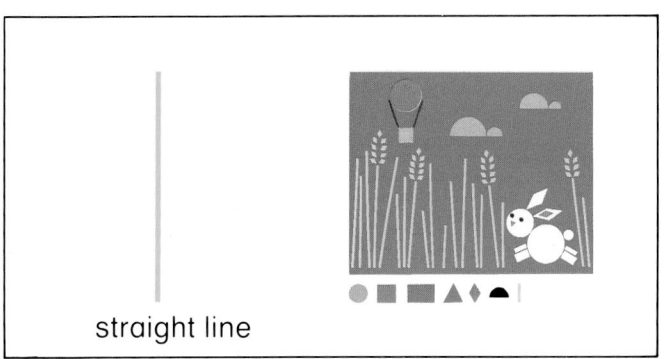

straight line

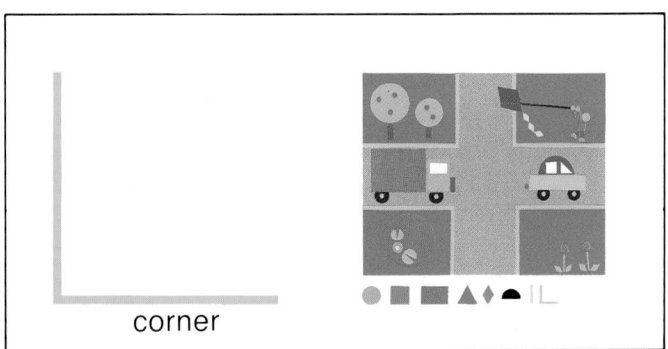

corner

zigzag line

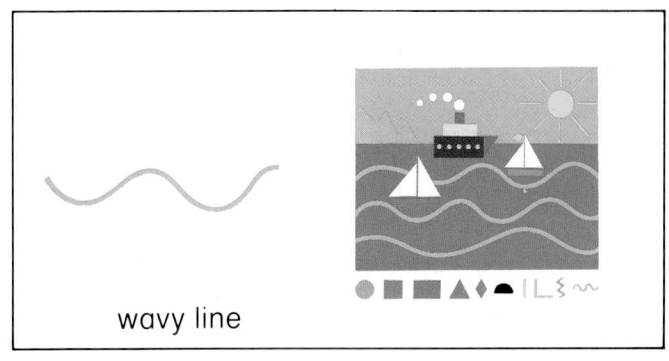

wavy line

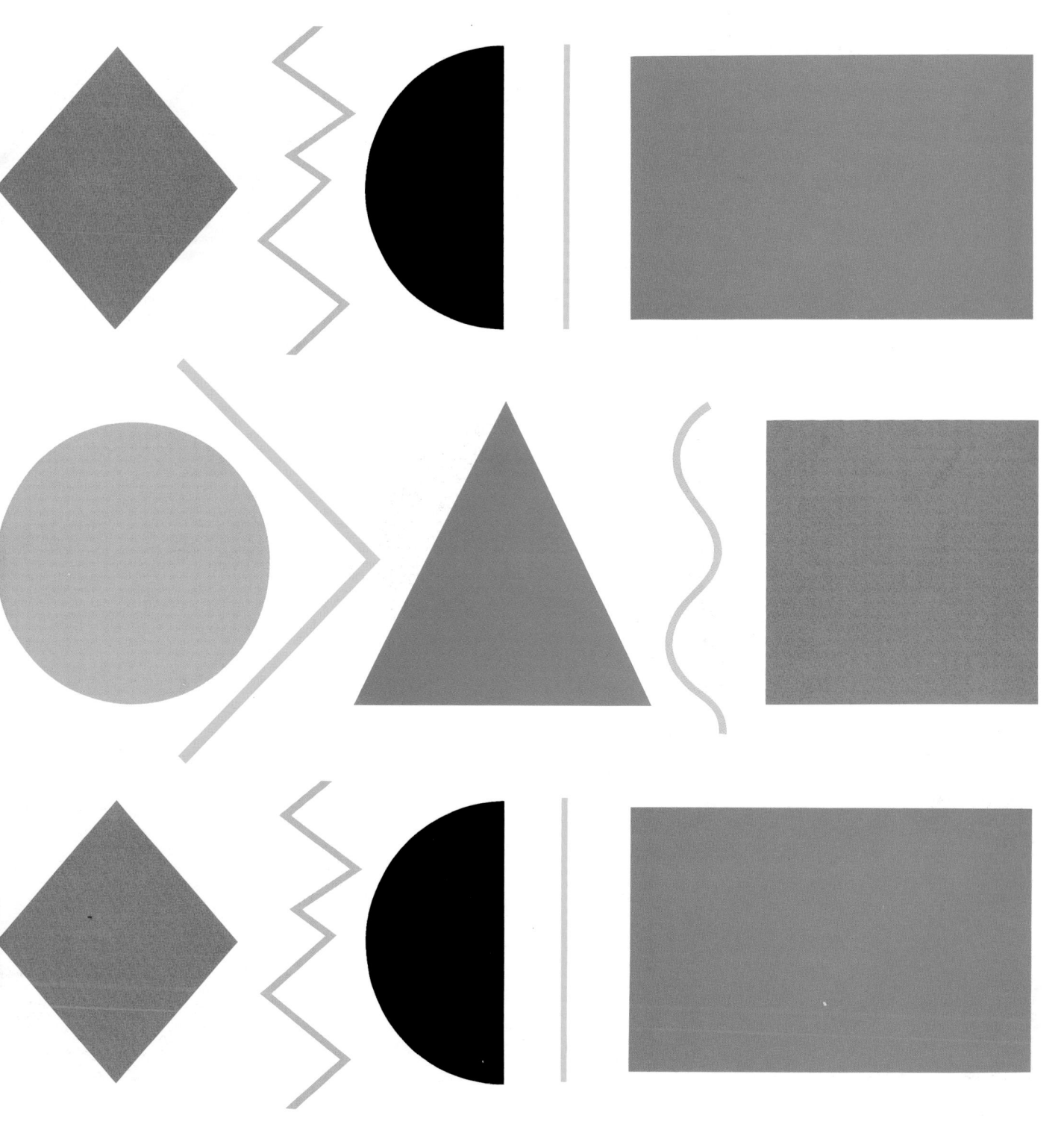